BUTTERFLIES

Anise Swallowtail
Papilio zelicaon
To 3 in. (8 cm)

Pale Tiger Swallowtail
Pterourus eurymedon
To 4 in. (10 cm)

Western Tiger Swallowtail
Papilio rutulus
To 4 in. (10 cm)

Cabbage White
Pieris rapae
To 2 in. (5 cm)

California Dogface
Zerene eurydice
To 2.5 in. (6 cm)
Note poodle-head pattern on forewings. **California's state butterfly.**

Sara Orangetip
Anthocharis sara
To 1.5 in. (4 cm)

Silvery Blue
Glaucopsyche lygdamus
To 1.25 in. (3.2 cm)

Cloudless Sulphur
Phoebis sennae
To 3 in. (8 cm)

Mourning Cloak
Nymphalis antiopa
To 3.5 in. (9 cm)

Monarch
Danaus plexippus
To 4 in. (10 cm)
Note rows of white spots on edges of wings.

Buckeye
Junonia coenia
To 2.5 in. (6 cm)

Red Admiral
Vanessa atalanta
To 3 in. (8 cm)

Most illustrations show the adult male in breeding coloration. Colors and markings may be duller or absent during different seasons. The measurements denote the length of species from snout-bill to tail tip. Butterfly measurements denote wingspan. Illustrations are not to scale.

Waterford Press produces reference guides that introduce novices to nature, science, survival and outdoor recreation. Product information is featured on the website: www.waterfordpress.com

Text and illustrations © 2006, 2021 by Waterford Press Inc. All rights reserved.
Cover images © Shutterstock.
To order, call 800-434-2555. For permissions, or to share comments, e-mail editor@waterfordpress.com.
For information on custom-published products, call 800-434-2555 or e-mail info@waterfordpress.com.

Made in the USA

978-1-58355-314-5
ISBN
$7.95 U.S.
50795
9 781583 553145
UPC
8 84682 01047 8
10 9 8 7 6 5 4 3 2 1
210917

A POCKET NATURALIST® GUIDE

NATURE OF SAN FRANCISCO & THE BAY AREA

A Folding Pocket Guide to Familiar Animals & Plants

T0123962

TREES & SHRUBS

Douglas-Fir
Pseudotsuga menziesii
To 200 ft. (61 m)
Flat needles grow in a spiral around branchlets. Cones have 3-pointed bracts protruding between the scales.

Redwood
Sequoia sempervirens To 325 ft. (99 m)
Bark is fibrous. Cones are 1 in. (3 cm) long. The world's tallest trees. **California's state tree.**

Western Hemlock
Tsuga heterophylla To 150 ft. (46 m)
Tree droops at the tip. Flat needles grow from 2 sides of twigs, parallel to the ground.

Monterey Cypress
Cupressus macrocarpa To 80 ft. (24 m)
Flat-topped coastal tree. Leaves are scale-like. Small cones have 8-14 scales.

Pacific Willow
Salix lasiandra To 50 ft. (15 m)
Narrow leaves are green above, grayish below.

Bluegum Eucalyptus
Eucalyptus globulus
To 120 ft. (36.5 m)
Tree has long, hanging leaves and peeling bark.

Trembling Aspen
Populus tremuloides To 70 ft. (21 m)
Long-stemmed leaves rustle in the slightest breeze.

Fremont Cottonwood
Populus fremontii To 80 ft. (24 m)
Heart-shaped leaves have gently-toothed edges and flattened stems. Flowers are succeeded by cottony seeds.

California-laurel
Umbellularia californica To 80 ft. (24 m)
Narrow leaves exude spicy scent when crushed. Greenish berries ripen in autumn.

California Sycamore
Platanus racemosa To 80 ft. (24 m)
Star-shaped leaves and spiny 'buttonball' fruits are key field marks.

California Buckeye
Aesculus californica To 25 ft. (7.6 m)
Pinkish flowers bloom in erect clusters in spring. Fruit contains 1-2 seeds that have a light 'eye' spot.

Pacific Madrone
Arbutus menziesii To 80 ft. (24 m)
Red-brown bark continuously peels away, exposing smooth inner bark.

WILDFLOWERS

English Daisy
Bellis perennis
To 8 in. (20 cm)
Common lawn weed.

Yarrow
Achillea millefolium
To 3 ft. (90 cm)
Leaves are fern-like.

White Trillium
Trillium ovatum
To 16 in. (40 cm)
Large 3-petalled flower is framed by a whorl of 3 broad leaves.

Mouse Ear Chickweed
Cerastium arvense
To 20 in. (50 cm)
White flowers have 5 notched petals.

Cow Parsnip
Heracleum lanatum
To 9 ft. (2.7 m)
Grows in moist soils. Creamy white flowers bloom in dense, flattened clusters.

Beach Strawberry
Fragaria chiloensis
Stems to 8 in. (20 cm)
Creeping plant.

Blue-eyed Grass
Sisyrinchium spp.
To 20 in. (50 cm)

Miniature Lupine
Lupinus bicolor
To 16 in. (40 cm)
Note star-shaped leaves.

Seaside Daisy
Erigeron glaucus
To 16 in. (40 cm)

American Vetch
Vicia americana
Stems to 7 ft. (2.1 m) long.
Climbing vine.

Baby Blue Eyes
Nemophila menziesii
To 12 in. (30 cm)
Petals are darkly speckled.

Mission Bells
Fritillaria lanceolata
To 40 in. (1 m)

Creamcup
Platystemon californicus
To 12 in. (30 cm)

Yellow Monkeyflower
Mimulus guttatus
To 3 ft. (90 cm)

Common Mullein
Verbascum thapsus
To 7 ft. (2.1 m)
Common roadside weed.

WILDFLOWERS

Common Sunflower
Helianthus annuus
To 9 ft. (2.7 m)
Flowers follow the sun across the sky each day.

California Poppy
Eschscholzia californica californica
To 2 ft. (60 cm)
Leaves are fern-like. **California's state flower.**

Tarweed
Madia elegans
To 4 ft. (1.2 m)

Blazing Star
Mentzelia spp.
To 5 ft. (1.5 m)
Flower has a central puff of long stamens.

Yellow Sand Verbena
Abronia latifolia
Stems to 3 ft. (90 cm)
Creeping beach plant.

Western Columbine
Aquilegia formosa
To 3 ft. (90 cm)
Flowers have long spurs.

Purple Owl Clover
Orthocarpus purpurea
To 15 in. (38 cm)

Farewell-to-Spring
Clarkia amoena
To 3 ft. (90 cm)

Indian Paintbrush
Castilleja spp.
To 3 ft. (90 cm)

Fireweed
Chamerion angustifolium
To 10 ft. (3 m)
Common in open woodlands and waste areas.

California Rhododendron
Rhododendron macrophyllum
To 25 ft. (7.6 m)
Flowering shrub.

Thistle
Cirsium spp.
To 5 ft. (1.5 m)
Leaves are scalloped and prickly.

Redwood Sorrel
Oxalis oregana
To 7 in. (18 cm)
Note clover-like leaves.

Beach Morning Glory
Calystegia soldanella
Stems to 20 in. (50 cm) long.
Creeping plant.

Shooting Star
Dodecatheon pulchellum
To 16 in. (40 cm)

MARINE LIFE

Dungeness Crab
Cancer magister
To 9 in. (23 cm)

Purple Shore Crab
Hemigrapsus nudus
To 2.5 in. (6 cm)

Fiddler Crab
Uca spp.
To 1.5 in. (4 cm)

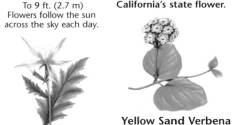

Pacific Littleneck Clam
Protothaca staminea
To 3 in. (8 cm)

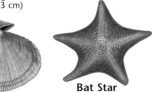

Bat Star
Patiria miniata
To 8 in. (20 cm)
May be red-brown to reddish.

Purple Sea Urchin
Strongylocentrotus purpuratus
To 4 in. (10 cm)

Pacific Razor Clam
Siliqua patula
To 7 in. (18 cm)

Ochre Sea Star
Pisaster ochraceus
To 20 in. (50 cm)
May be red, purple, orange or brown.

Giant Green Anemone
Anthopleura xanthogrammica
To 12 in. (30 cm)

California Horn Snail
Cerithidea californica
To 1.75 in. (4.5 cm)

California Mussel
Mytilus californianus
To 10 in. (25 cm)

Giant Western Nassa
Nassarius fossatus
To 2 in. (5 cm)

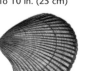

Barnacle
Balanus spp. To 3 in. (8 cm)
Grows in clusters attached to rocks and piers.

Nuttal's Cockle
Clinocardium nuttallii
To 6 in. (15 cm)

Sand Dollar
Dendraster excentricus
To 3 in. (8 cm)

BEACH DRIFT

Sea Urchin Skeleton

Sand Dollar Skeleton

Dogfish Egg Case

Western Pond Turtle
Clemmys marmorata To 7 in. (18 cm)
Common in vegetated ponds and lakes.

Red-eared Slider
Trachemys scripta elegans
To 11 in. (28 cm)

Pacific Gopher Snake
Pituophis catenifer catenifer
To 8 ft. (2.4 m)

California Red-sided Garter Snake
Thamnophis sirtalis infernalis
To 4 ft. (1.2 m)
Note red bars on sides.

Western Skink
Plestiodon skiltonianus
To 9 in. (23 cm)
Has 4 light body stripes.

California Toad
Anaxyrus boreas halophilus
To 4 in. (10 cm)
Males have a soft, clucking call.

Bullfrog
Lithobates catesbeianus
To 8 in. (20 cm)
Call is a deep-pitched – jug-o-rum.

Pacific Treefrog
Pseudacris regilla
To 2 in. (5 cm)
Color ranges from brown to green. Note dark eye stripe. Call is 2-part – kreck-ek – with the last syllable rising.

California Newt
Taricha torosa To 8 in. (20 cm)
Red-brown skin is warty.

BIRDS

Eared Grebe
Podiceps nigricollis
To 14 in. (35 cm)
Note black neck and golden ear tufts.

Pied-billed Grebe
Podilymbus podiceps
To 13 in. (33 cm)
Note banded white bill.

Western Grebe
Aechmophorus occidentalis
To 25 in. (63 cm)

Ruddy Duck
Oxyura jamaicensis
To 16 in. (40 cm)
Note cocked tail.

Mallard
Anas platyrhynchos To 28 in. (70 cm)

Cinnamon Teal
Spatula cyanoptera To 17 in. (43 cm)

Northern Pintail
Anas acuta To 29 in. (73 cm)

Wood Duck To 20 in. (50 cm)
Aix sponsa

Common Goldeneye
Bucephala clangula
To 20 in. (50 cm)

American Coot
Fulica americana
To 16 in. (40 cm)

Surf Scoter
Melanitta perspicillata
To 20 in. (50 cm)
Note white patches on nape and forehead.

Canvasback
Aythya valisineria To 2 ft. (60 cm)
Note sloping forehead and black bill.

Double-crested Cormorant
Phalacrocorax auritus
To 3 ft. (90 cm)
Note orange-yellow throat patch.

Brown Pelican
Pelecanus occidentalis
To 50 in. (1.3 m)

Canada Goose
Branta canadensis
To 45 in. (1.14 m)

Great Blue Heron
Ardea herodias
To 4.5 ft. (1.4 m)

Great Egret
Ardea alba
To 38 in. (95 cm)
Note yellow bill and black feet.

Black-crowned Night-Heron
Nycticorax nycticorax
To 28 in. (70 cm)

Black-necked Stilt
Himantopus mexicanus
To 17 in. (43 cm)

Killdeer
Charadrius vociferus
To 12 in. (30 cm)
Note two breast bands.

Sanderling
Calidris alba
To 8 in. (20 cm)
Runs in and out with waves along shorelines.

Snowy Egret
Egretta thula
To 26 in. (65 cm)
Note black bill and yellow feet.

Black Oystercatcher
Haematopus bachmani
To 18 in. (45 cm)

Greater Yellowlegs
Tringa melanoleuca
To 15 in. (38 cm)
Call is a 3-5 note whistle.

Western Sandpiper
Calidris mauri
To 7 in. (18 cm)

American Avocet
Recurvirostra americana
To 20 in. (50 cm)

Least Tern
Sternula antillarum
To 10 in. (25 cm)
Note small size and yellow bill.

Long-billed Curlew
Numenius americanus
To 26 in. (65 cm)
Long bill is slightly downturned.

Anna's Hummingbird
Calypte anna
To 4 in. (10 cm)
Note red throat and crown.

California Gull
Larus californicus
To 23 in. (58 cm)
Note black and red spots on its bill.

Bonaparte's Gull
Chroicocephalus philadelphia
To 14 in. (35 cm)

California Quail
Callipepla californica
To 10 in. (25 cm)

Belted Kingfisher
Megaceryle alcyon
To 14 in. (35 cm)

Northern Harrier
Circus hudsonius
To 22 in. (55 cm)
Note white rump.

Turkey Vulture
Cathartes aura
To 32 in. (80 cm)
Note red head and two-toned underwings.

Red-tailed Hawk
Buteo jamaicensis
To 23 in. (63 cm)

Great Horned Owl
Bubo virginianus
To 25 in. (63 cm)
Call is a resonant – hoo-HOO-hoooo.

Rock Pigeon
Columba livia
To 13 in. (33 cm)

Mourning Dove
Zenaida macroura
To 13 in. (33 cm)
Call is a mournful – ooah-woo-woo-woo.

California Thrasher
Toxostoma redivivum
To 12 in. (30 cm)

Red-breasted Nuthatch
Sitta canadensis
To 4.5 in. (11 cm)

Black Phoebe
Sayornis nigricans
To 7 in. (18 cm)

Northern Flicker
Colaptes auratus
To 13 in. (33 cm)
Wing and tail linings are red.

Downy Woodpecker
Dryobates pubescens
To 6 in. (15 cm)
The similar hairy woodpecker is larger and has a longer bill.

Violet-green Swallow
Tachycineta thalassina
To 6 in. (15 cm)

Oak Titmouse
Baeolophus inornatus
To 6 in. (15 cm)
Note head crest.

Chestnut-backed Chickadee
Poecile rufescens
To 5 in. (13 cm)

Cedar Waxwing
Bombycilla cedrorum
To 7 in. (18 cm)
Red wing marks look like waxy droplets.

Marsh Wren
Cistothorus palustris
To 5 in. (13 cm)
Note white stripes on back and white eyebrow stripe.

Western Bluebird
Sialia mexicana
To 7 in. (18 cm)

California Scrub-Jay
Aphelocoma californica
To 13 in. (33 cm)

Steller's Jay
Cyanocitta stelleri
To 14 in. (35 cm)

American Robin
Turdus migratorius
To 11 in. (28 cm)

Brown-headed Cowbird
Molothrus ater
To 7 in. (18 cm)

Brewer's Blackbird
Euphagus cyanocephalus
To 9 in. (23 cm)

European Starling
Sturnus vulgaris
To 8 in. (20 cm)

Red-winged Blackbird
Agelaius phoeniceus
To 9 in. (23 cm)

Northern Mockingbird
Mimus polyglottos
To 11 in. (28 cm)

American Crow
Corvus brachyrhynchos
To 22 in. (55 cm)
Call is a distinct – caw.

Spotted Towhee
Pipilo maculatus
To 9 in. (23 cm)

American Goldfinch
Spinus tristis
To 5 in. (13 cm)

California Towhee
Melozone crissalis
To 10 in. (25 cm)

White-crowned Sparrow
Zonotrichia leucophrys
To 8 in. (20 cm)
White crown is bordered by black stripes.

Bullock's Oriole
Icterus bullockii
To 8 in. (20 cm)

Yellow-rumped Warbler
Setophaga coronata
To 6 in. (15 cm)
Note yellow on rump and crown. Throat is yellow or white.
'Myrtle' Race
'Audubon' Race

House Finch
Haemorhous mexicanus
To 6 in. (15 cm)

Dark-eyed Junco
Junco hyemalis
To 7 in. (18 cm)
Four related 'races' all have a dark hood and light outer tail feathers.

House Sparrow
Passer domesticus
To 6 in. (15 cm)

Virginia Opossum
Didelphis virginiana
To 40 in. (1 m)
Note long fur and naked tail.

Western Gray Squirrel
Sciurus griseus
To 23 in. (58 cm)

California Ground Squirrel
Otospermophilus beecheyi
To 20 in. (50 cm)

Brush Rabbit
Sylvilagus bachmani
To 15 in. (38 cm)

Black-tailed Jackrabbit
Lepus californicus
To 25 in. (63 cm)

Norway Rat
Rattus norvegicus
To 18 in. (45 cm)

Chipmunk
Neotamias spp.
To 12 in. (30 cm)
Note white stripes on side and face.

Deer Mouse
Peromyscus maniculatus
To 8 in. (20 cm)

Common Muskrat
Ondatra zibethicus
To 2 ft. (60 cm)
Aquatic rodent has a naked, scaly tail.

Gray Fox
Urocyon cinereoargenteus
To 3.5 ft. (1.1 m)
Note black-tipped tail.

Striped Skunk
Mephitis mephitis
To 32 in. (80 cm)

Common Raccoon
Procyon lotor
To 40 in. (1 m)

Coyote
Canis latrans To 52 in. (1.3 m)
Note bushy, black-tipped tail.

California Sea Lion
Zalophus californianus
To 8 ft. (2.4 m)
Note domed skull.

Mule Deer
Odocoileus hemionus
To 7.5 ft. (2.3 m)

Harbor Seal
Phoca vitulina
To 6 ft. (1.8 m)